THE DIGITAL SUPERHERO

DISCOVER KITSU'S BLOCKCHAIN, NFT AND CRYPTOASSETS ADVENTURES IN THE ALGO WORLD

KITSUNE INU ASA

CONTENTS

CHAPTER ONE

The world was in chaos, the streets were empty, and everyone was suffering from trilemma. Betty sat on the porch steps of her house and watched the skinny-looking rats run across the streets. Betty sighed deeply; she saw Mrs. Brentwood walking out of her house. The older woman was carrying a bag of cans; Betty ran across the street to help Mrs. Brentwood. "Good morning, Mrs. Brentwood" Betty smiled; the helm of her dress caught a nail last week; Betty almost tripped as she climbed the steps to join Mrs. Brentwood on the porch. "Good morning, Betty" Mrs. Brentwood gave Betty a pat on the head. "Bring that dress later, so I can fix it," Mrs. Brentwood added. "It caught a nail when I went to pick some flowers on the field," Betty explained. "Flowers? I didn't know we have any left," Mrs. Brentwood said. "If you climb up the mountain, you could find some good ones," Betty answered. Since the beginning of the trilemma, all the good plants had died, and people could barely feed themselves.

Mrs. Brentwood looked at her dead garden, the flowers were dried up, and there was nothing other than dead soil sitting in the flower pot. The pollution in the air couldn't make anything grow; it was difficult to get fresh air. "Will this ever be over?" Betty asked. "Very soon," Mrs. Brentwood assured the young girl. She had no idea if she was going to live to see that day. Mrs. Brentwood closed her eyes and remembered the days when she hosted a big family dinner; the children were always expectant. She hasn't seen any of her kids since the trilemma started, and gradually Mrs. Brentwood was losing faith in the system. But she couldn't tell Betty that their world was crashing; the young girl could not be discouraged.

M r. Peter was in his office when the phone on his desk started buzzing; he picked up the receiver immediately. "Riley, what is it?" Mr. Peter glanced at his watch; he was running late for a meeting with the board. "The Research team in Portland said it's urgent," Riley answered. "This better be important; I'm running late for an important meeting. Put them on," Mr. Peter sighed. The Astrological and Space Agency is an international agency, and the office is situated in Arizona. The agency has a lot of research teams across the world; this is the first time Peter is speaking with the team in Portland. He was made a Director a year ago.

"Good morning, Mr. Peter" the person on the line had a very subtle voice. "Good morning" Peter's reply was curt. "I'm Professor Nasir, and I'm with one of my researchers here, Mr. Richard." The Professor was still into introductions, but Peter was growing impatient. "I'm sorry, but can we just cut to the chase; I'm late for an important meeting," Peter replied. "I'm sorry for the inconvenience. We received some signals this morning that is a bit unsettling," Professor Nasir explained. "What do you mean?" Peter was listening with rapt attention this time. "The signals we received this morning show that the world is going to be hit by a trilemma," Professor Nasir answered. "Trilemma?" Peter glanced at his watch. "Yes, sir, we can't find the ozone layer; it's almost like it disappeared." Professor Nasir explained. "What do you mean, you can't find it?" Peter was trying hard not to panic. "You can re-run the status over there. The disappearance of the ozone layer is going to cause environmental pollution, which will definitely affect the economic stability of the world. If we can get food, and I don't know what to expect," Professor Nasir sighed deeply. "This is a disaster. Professor Nasir, this information is classified. Put a lid on it; I'll get back to you," Peter dropped the receiver.

"Riley, I'm heading to the research center," Peter said as he picked his car keys. "Sir, what about the meeting?" Riley looked confused. "I'll call the Chairman of the board from the car. Whatever information that comes from Portland is placed on the priority list, and please get Professor Nasir down here" Peter rushed out of his office. As he turned the ignition of the car, he wondered how much time they had left before the trilemma began. The exhaust from his car was definitely going to contribute a whole lot, but it was for a worthy cause. Peter called the Chairman of the board in his car; Mrs. Hilary picked up on the second ring. "So nice of you to keep us waiting," she said. "We have bigger issues to deal with; I just got a call from the research team in Portland. The ozone layer is gone, and there is an impending disaster" Peter didn't mince words. "You're joking, right?" Mrs. Hilary sounded frantic. "I wish was" Peter drove into the parking lot. "What does that mean?" Mrs. Hilary asked. "Pollution, climate change, and eventually, poverty. It is called the trilemma," Peter answered. "How long do we have?" Mrs. Hilary's voice was almost like a whisper. "That's what I'm about to find out," Peter replied. "I'll inform the board," Mrs. Hillary said before she dropped the call.

Peter got out of his car in a rush; the research team had a standard facility in Arizona. A big room that could comfortably accommodate seventy researchers. The room was furnished with recent technological devices and large screens that projected the relevant information for display. The head of the research team met Peter had the door. "I wasn't expecting you...." Professor Slovaks was a renowned person in the field, and it only made sense that he was the head of the team. "I need eyes on the ozone layer," Peter said as he walked into the room. The image was projected on the screen, and Peter ran his fingers through his hair. "What is this?" Professor Slovaks adjusted his wide-rimmed glasses. Peter stared at the screen in shock. "It's gone" dead silence fell upon the room. If a pin dropped, everyone would hear it. "This is not good. Walter, I need visuals from outer space," Professor Slovaks shouted. The footage appeared on the screen, and everyone could see a big black object; in the shape of a ball advancing towards the earth. "Is that heading for the earth?" Peter asked the question everyone was afraid to ask. "Yes," Professor Slovaks answered wide-eyed. "How long do we have?" Peter asked as he paced the room. "It's traveling 0.58km per hour. Give or take, we have a week before it touches earth," one of the researchers answered.

"What is the worst-case scenario?" Peter stared at Professor Slovaks for an answer. "There is no limit to this thing," Professor Slovaks sighed. "Find proactive measure or something that can stop the trilemma" Peter was heading for the door. "This thing is inevitable," Professor Slovaks replied. "Then find coping mechanisms," Peter said as he left the room. As he walked back to his car, he wondered if there was going to be a way out. The world was coming to an end, and no one saw it coming. Peter got into the car and leaned his head against the steering wheel. His phone was buzzing; Peter checked the caller ID and answered the phone call. "Peter, how long do we have?" it was Mrs. Hilary on the phone. "A week," Peter answered flatly. "Can we stop this?"

Mrs. Hilary asked. "Not before it hits us" Peter was scared of the words that proceeded out of his mouth. "I'll speak to the Secretary-General of the United Nations immediately," Mrs. Hilary sighed. "We should all be prepared," Peter answered. "Do me a favor, bring that team to Arizona. If they discovered this crisis first before we did, then they must be thinking of a solution now," Mrs. Hilary said.

Peter sighed deeply after Mrs. Hilary ended the call. The woman was right; the Portland team may have a way out. Peter returned to his office; Riley was on her feet immediately he walked in. "Sir, is it true?" Riley looked like she was going to cry; Peter had never seen the lady so worried. "I'm afraid it is," Peter replied. "Oh! No," Riley gasped. "When will Professor Nasir arrive?" Peter asked as he sat on his chair. "He should have boarded the plane already; he should be here in the next four hours" Riley glanced at her wristwatch. "1600hrs, to be precise," Riley added. "That's good. Get him to me the minute he touches the base." Peter replied. "I also need you to set up a meeting with all members of staff and a press conference for briefing," Peter said as he leaned back into the chair. "We are holding a press conference?" Riley asked. "Everyone should be aware; this thing might take us unaware," Peter answered. Riley went into execution mode the minute she stepped out of Peter's office.

Professor Nasir was taken to the Astrological and Space Agency from the airport. Peter was going to brief the press after meeting with Professor Nasir. Peter met the Professor at the door, "Good evening, Professor Nasir" Peter stretched out his hand, and the man took it in a firm grip. "It's an honor to be here, sir," said Professor Nasir. "Well, I wish it was a different situation; maybe I would have given you a tour," Peter said as they walked into his office. "I understand," Professor Nasir answered. "Please sit," Peter said as he sat on his seat. "So, what are we dealing with here?" Peter leaned back into the chair. "We came up with a theory in Portland. We believe that the ozone layer has been completely worn out previously. Our team discovered that what was left was a thin layer. Like I explained on the phone, at 1800hrs yesterday, one of our researchers discovered that the ozone was completely eradicated. Whatever you saw is heading straight for the earth, and I don't know how much time we have left." Professor Nasir explained. "One week" Peter's voice was almost like a whisper. "Sorry?" Professor Nasir didn't hear Peter speak. "We have one week to stop this thing, or it is going to consume us," Peter answered. The room grew silent, and it felt like a judge gave a death sentence. "Do you have a solution?" Peter knew he was treading on quicksand with that question. "On our end, we are trying to work something out, and I'm sure the other teams are trying to do the same thing. But I don't think there will be any solution before the week runs out. We'll have to run a couple of tests, and you know how long that can take," Professor Nasir sighed. "For now, I need all hands on deck" Peter rose to his feet. "I have a press briefing in a few minutes. I think it's best everyone is aware." Peter added. "I just got off the phone with the

Chairman of the Board, the UN secretary-general has authorized the press briefing. The Chairman said I should also inform you that the Secretary-General received the news in shock" Riley reeled out like an answering machine. "We're all in shock. Professor Nasir, you're coming with me. Your team saw this impending danger; first, you know more than I do," Peter said as he walked out of the room.

The pressmen were in the lobby of the facility; they looked like hungry sharks. As Peter stepped into the hall, the flashlight from their cameras almost blinded him. He hated briefings, but it turned out he didn't have a choice on a day like this. "Good morning, I will just be here to drop a few information, and I will be out of your hair" the room grew silent as Peter started talking; the only sound that could be heard was the clicking buttons of the camera and the keyboard of their computer. "The earth is about to be hit by something we call the trilemma; at 0800hrs today, we confirmed that the ozone layer is completely worn out. Professor Nasir here, whose team in Portland discovered this impending disaster first would give us the details" Peter turned to Professor Nasir. The man looked like he was going to faint, but he managed to compose himself; Peter didn't even notice that the room had gone totally silent. Professor Nasir cleared his throat. "In Portland, a researcher in my team noticed that a big giant ball of direct UV emissions is heading towards earth, and that was when they discovered that the ozone layer was completely gone. The trilemma means that we are going to be experiencing climate change, pollution and this will also give rise to poverty. The pollution in the environment will make it difficult for plants and animals to grow properly, so we may be experiencing famine, and we can longer predict the weather. Professor Nasir explained. The reporters stared at the Professor in shock, "How long do we have before the trilemma hits us?" one of the reporters asked. "Give or take a week," Peter answered. "We would also like to inform the general public that it is best to store up your houses with enough food items before the trilemma starts. But we assure you that we are working on a solution" Peter left the podium band Professor Nasir was right behind him. Even the reporters didn't have the strength to shout and ask questions. The duo just delivered a life-changing press statement.

Peter wasn't ready for the change, but he had no choice; it was taking them unaware, and there was nothing anyone could do about it. Professor Slovaks had eyes on the trilemma, and he informed Pete that it was closing in and would earth anytime soon. Peter sighed; maybe the human race was going into extinction, but they still had to make an effort to stop the destroyer.

Mr. Peter walked into the office; the place was deserted. The building was bustling with life a year ago. The Astrological and Space Agency had become a shadow of itself. Even Miss Riley at the desk wasn't looking like her old self. Mr. Peter could notice the stitch on her dress. "Good morning, Mr. Peter," Riley said as she opened the door to his office. "Good morning, Riley," Peter answered. "You know, you don't have to come to work" Peter dropped his weather-beaten bag on the table. "I don't have anything to do at home, and I love the distraction. We can't watch TV, and we can't even use our mobile phones, so we don't cause more damage. It's like somebody cast a spell on the earth and sent us back to the primitive stage" Riley sighed. "We'll learn to live like this," Peter said as he took off his jacket. "I don't think that's a problem anymore. We've been living like this for the past three years. If you ask me, we are doing just fine" Riley shrugged. "That's the attitude" Peter tried to smile. "I don't think so, Mr. Peter. I'm pretty sure I'll give up soon. My neighbor and her children died of hunger yesterday, and it was devastating. I really wish I could help, but I couldn't. Honestly, I don't even know how long I have. Some people, however, have the privilege of buying fresh air in cans because they spend the last days before the trilemma stashing public funds enough to feed a thousand-person for years. Now, how is that fair?" Riley sighed. "We can't give up just yet. So let's focus on today's business," Peter said as he leaned back in his chair. The landline on his desk was ringing, and Peter stared at the phone with surprise. It has been ages since anyone called the office line. Riley picked up the phone with excitement, "Dr. Peter's office, please, who is on the line?" Riley asked politely. "Professor Nasir, can I speak to the Director?" the man asked. "Hold on, one minute. I will put on the line," Riley answered.

"Who is it?" Peter asked with zero interest. "It's Professor Nasir," Riley answered. "What?" Riley handed the man the phone. "Professor... Nasir?" Peter stuttered. "Good morning, Director," the Professor answered. "I don't even know what time of the day it is; I think it's morning, but there is a thick black fog aside, which makes me confused," Peter answered. "I have some news," Professor Nasir replied. "What is the worst thing that can happen after this?" Peter sighed. "We may have found a solution," Professor Nasir answered. "One thing I'm not willing to do is to raise my hopes" Peter was drumming his fingers on the table. "I thought so too, but after giving it a lot of consideration, this could work," Professor Nasir answered. "Then I want this information to be classified; no other soul outside your team should hear it" Peter sat upright in his chair immediately. "What's the solution?" Peter asked. "We've been working on a noble premium called 'Silvio,'" Professor Nasir answered. "I'm listening" Peter was paying rapt attention. "Silvio is a digital entity that had a mind of his own, and his thinking capabilities is more than that of ten men. Silvio was designed to solve the issue of decentralized funds, scalability, and security. In fact, Silvio is our only shot at the trilemma," Professor Nasir explained. "You're telling me you guys in Portland created an artificial intelligence in the midst of this wreck?" Peter was impressed. "It was either that, or we would wait till the human nature enters into extinction," Professor Nasir answered. "So, how is Silvio going to help us from this mess?" Peter asked. "We'll have to wait. He's an AI, but I'm confident he will come up with something," Professor Nasir assured the Director. "That's fine; I just hope it doesn't take years," Peter answered before he dropped the call. "Silvio is super smart; it shouldn't take that long," Professor Nasir replied confidently. "Your words against mine," Peter said as he dropped the received. Peter had learned not to be hopeful; in the past three years, he has received calls just like this, and nothing changed. "It may work this time" Riley didn't sound like she believed her own words. "Remember BTC?" Peter asked. "Ah… I sincerely thought that was our savior," Riley answered.

Professor Slovaks called Peter that morning; Peter was desperate for solutions. So Professor Slovaks call was welcomed with so much joy. "Good morning, Director" Slovaks sounded confident. "Good morning, Professor Slovaks," Peter answered. "We may have stumbled on a solution," Professor Slovaks replied. "What?" Peter jumped out of his chair. "I'm coming down there. I want to hear all about it." Peter rushed to grab his car key from the table. "Sir…?" Riley almost bumped into the Director at the door. "Professor Slovaks thinks they found a solution," Peter said as he rushed out. "Oh! Thank goodness. I'm currently out of funds" Riley sighed.

Peter arrived in Arizona; he had to take his car, which was something he hadn't done in a long while. The earth was already in a mess, and he didn't want to endanger the earth more they had collectively done. If it was going to be a solution, then driving to Arizona was a risk he was willing to take. As he drove on the highway, Peter couldn't help but notice some women and their children walking on the highway. They were covered in soot, and the children looked malnourished. The farm girls were covered with dark soot, and the sun was very harsh on their skin. One of the children could barely walk on the tarred road, which was scalding hot. Peter could feel their pain and despair; he realized how the trilemma had put a lot of people in pain. It was the consequences of their own negligence, but there had to be a way out of the trilemma. Thankfully, Professor Slovaks had found one. Peter stepped on the gas and arrived at the research center soon enough. He met Professor Slovaks in the parking lot; Peter's car was the only car in the big parking lot. "I'm surprised you still have gas," Professor Slovaks said as he shook hands with the Director. "I stored up gas for emergencies situations just like this one," Peter answered.

"So, what do we have here?" Peter and the Professor walked into the building. "It's called BTC. With your permission, we are preparing to launch it as soon as possible." Professor Slovaks answered. "If this thing works, then prepare to launch" Peter could feel the blood rushing in his body. "That's great. The BTC is to reactivate the redistribution of wealth and also provide more oxygen for the people. We should see green in the next few months," Professor Slovaks explained. "To think I hate green and now my whole depends on the amount of green that we have left on earth," Peter said as they walked into the control room. On the screen, the BTC was projected, "So, how do we launch this thing?" Peter asked. "We are sending it into the outer space with our rockets ships," Professor

Slovaks answered. "Then what happens next?" Peter asked. "When appropriately positioned in the space, it activates an orb around the planet that protects the death from the UV rays in the space," Professor Slovaks answered. "What's the worst that could happen?" Peter asked. "At this point, there is no risk that is not worth taking," Professor Slovaks answered. "That's my thought exactly," Peter replied.

"Let's launch it," Peter answered. "Let's launch the BTC," Professor Slovaks said to the room, and the news was welcomed with a deafening round of applause. Peter watched the screen as the rocket ship was preparing to be launched from the rocket ship. His eyes were fixed on the screen till the BTC disassembled and planted itself in the space. "When will it create the orb?" Peter asked. "It should take a day or two, but we'll be on the lookout," Professor Slovaks answered. While Peter and the Professor were still when something hit the BTC satellite. "What was that?" Peter turned around quickly. The control room had lost footage. "What going on?" Professor Slovaks shouted. "I think we lost the camera; we are running blindly here, sir," a guy with wide-rimmed glasses sitting at the front of a computer answered. "You know we have to monitor the progress of the BTC!" Professor Slovaks was obviously on edge. "Get some cameras up there as soon as fast as you can" Professor Slovaks heart was racing. Peter paced the room, hoping that the BTC satellite had not been destroyed.

After several days of trying, the team was able to get a

camera to the space. But the feedback wasn't what they expected. The BTC activation was not progressive; the orb was slow and could only cover some parts of the globe. "How long is it going to take?" Peter asked. "I have no idea" Professor Slovaks sounded perplexed. "So what you're saying is we're going to have to settle with this little arc" Peter threw his hands up in the air. "I can guarantee you that this is not the result we anticipated," Professor Slovaks. "It will take years before this orb is completed! That is if there is no malfunction" Peter sounded exasperated. He saw the disappointed look on the faces of the people who have worked tirelessly to find a solution and realized they had just tried their best and failed. "It's okay, everyone. Let's just move on," Peter said as he walked out of the room. Peter needed some fresh air, but the air wasn't fresh anymore. He walked to the top of the building, the sky was dark, and Peter couldn't even tell if it was going to rain or not. The land looked scorched, and there was no green vegetation to admire. Everything looked bland, and life lost its color.

Peter heard footsteps walking towards him; he turned to see who. "I'm so sorry. We really thought we had things under control" there was a long bead of sweat on the Professor's lip. "I understand" Peter knew how much everyone wanted it to work. "The BTC has created a safe haven for some people in Antarctica. If you ask me, that's a good thing. It's just so slow; we don't know how long it's going to take or if it's going to ever make round the globe" Peter sighed. "That's something I don't want to be reminded of," Professor

Slovaks replied. "At least we know the human race is not going to go into extinction" Peter smiled. "That's on the lighter note," Professor Slovaks answered. "But the impact the trilemma has on the universe would take out 80% of the human creation," Peter said. "I don't know how much time we have left," Professor Slovaks answered. "I guess we'll never know," Peter sighed.

CHAPTER TWO

L ily was in Canada when the trilemma started; she left her five-year-old daughter Betty with her husband in London. Lily was a specialist in cardiology; there was a patient who needed to have a heart transplant so, the hospital had to fly Lily into the country to perform the country. The ASA had delivered a press release that the ozone layer and that the earth was going to be hit by a massive dark ball heading straight for earth. They didn't know when it was going to happen, but their calculations were it was going to happen in a week. The plan was to rush into Canada and return quickly before the direct UV rays hit the earth. It was going to one quick stop, and she had time, but things didn't go as planned. The minute Lily finished the operation, the ball hit the earth. There was a deafening sound, and everywhere went black; miraculously, Lily's patient survived, and she was glad that she gave someone another chance to spend time with her family.

Lily didn't have that privileged, though; her husband and daughter were far away in London. Lily couldn't get to them, and it was frustrating. She tried to book a flight back home that night, but the airport wasn't working anymore, the cell phones weren't working, and it seemed like the world had come to an end. Lily tried so hard to get back home, but all her plans were futile. Some persons extorted her of the money she had left with a promise they were going to get her back to London. But it never happened, and Lily was eventually left penniless in Canada. Thank goodness for the hospital; some good people came to share food at the now dysfunctional hospital. Lily sat on one of the benches in the ward, the number of sick people had skyrocketed, and the hospital was understaffed. The environment was no longer habitable; it's only normal that people will fall sick. The pharmaceuticals companies were shit down, they couldn't get access to resources, and it was highly risky to release toxic fumes into the already polluted atmosphere. Lily wondered how much longer they could endure the hardship; it was the end. But even in the end, Lily wanted to be with family, but she couldn't, and that was devastating.

If only she could get out of Canada, but there was no way out; if anyone were found driving a car in the street, the people would attack such an individual for trying to destroy the glimmer of hope they had left. "Mrs. Brandon?" one of the young nurses walked towards Lily. "Ashely, I didn't expect to see you here today" Lily was feeling a bit woozy. "I got tired of sitting at home and waiting for all of these to end" Ashely threw her hands in the air. "I hope it ends soon," Lily sighed. "Do you really think it is going to end?" Ashely asked. "I don't know; we just have to hope that it ends one day" Lily shrugged. "How is that going to happen?" Ashely stared at Lily. "I have no idea. I just want to be with my family," Lily cried, her voice traveling throughout the entire hall. The room was dead silent, and it was almost like nobody moved. "It's okay, Lily" Ashely gave her a gentle rub on the back. "My family would be worried sick; I promised them I was going to be back the next day. I had no idea that the next day was going to be chaos." Lilly sniffled. "I think you need to stop putting too much thought into it," Ashely advised. "You do not know what I'm feeling," Lily retorted. "Well, I know this isn't going to get you out of Canada," Ashely answered. Ashley's words rang a bell in Lily's ears; she inhaled deeply and leaned back on the chair.

"I know how you've been feeling, but I think I know something that will get you out of this trench," Ashely whispered.

"You do?" Lily moved closer to the nurse; it was apparent she didn't want anybody to hear. "I heard it's very expensive but trust me, that's your only ticket out of this place," Ashely continued. "I'm all ears," Lily listened with rapt attention. "Ethereum," Ashely said with a low voice. "Ethereum?" Lily stared at the girl blankly. Ashely gave her a slight nod. "The news is that there is a habitable place in Antarctica, but you cannot get in there without ETH," Ashely explained. "I don't know how true that is; I just want to go home," Lily replied. "The privileged ones are creating a safe haven for themselves with Ethereum," Ashely answered. "How is that even possible, Ashely?" Lily asked. "Well, I know not everybody is going to die," Ashley answered. Lily stared at the young nurse, this was a big risk, and the money was all she had left. "So, what do we do?" Lily asked quietly. "I will get more information then contact you; I heard they are going by sea," Ashley answered. "Sea, the water is contaminated; they wouldn't last a day out there," Lily gasped. "That's if you're going to Antarctica" Ashley rose to her feet as a young man was carried into the hospital. Lily watched the young nurse attend to the patient; Ashely was a nice young lady. Lily was worried that if Ashely's plan didn't work out, then she may never see her daughter. Lily sat on the chair, going over the details of their discussion. "Mrs. Brandon? I think I need your help" Ashley was kneeling in front of the man. "What is it?" Lily asked as she walked towards the group. "I think it's best you see it for yourself," Ashley replied. Lily examined the patient and told him to open his mouth; what she saw next sent her reeling backward. The man's throat was covered in black as if it was painted in black. "How long has he been outside?" Lily asked. "Over a month, he has no place to stay. So we live together in a shed," the woman standing next to him replied. "I understand you perfectly, but this is not going to be easy. We don't have any drugs, and we have to get the spot out of his system" Lily felt helpless.

"Let me see what I can do," Ashley said. "What can you possibly do?" Lily asked. "Since all we do is harmful to the environment, trying to save a dying person shouldn't hurt," Ashley replied. "Do you have any idea that we are all going to die in this trilemma at a point" Lily didn't see the need to save someone now when they were all going to die soon? There was no way anyone would survive from the trilemma anyway. From Lily's point of view, they were doing the man a huge favor if they let him die. "Just tell me what you need" Ashley was adamant. "I know you won't find any drugs. So clean water is my only option," Lily answered. "Clean water," Ashely sighed deeply before leaving the room. Lily watched the young nurse leave the room; if the Ethereum was going to get her home, then she had to give it a shot. Lily had never imagined that she would ever be in such a helpless situation. There was no harm in trying, but Lily's hope was that this time it would work out.

Betty sat in the dark living room; a small lamp by the couch was all the light they could afford. When the dilemma started, the government had put out a structure in controlling energy and waste. Betty's father left the house in the morning, and Betty was by herself. She saw her mother's portrait on the television; Betty could remember the day the picture was taken. The family had gone to the beach, and it was one of the happiest days of Betty's life. The sky was blue, and the birds were flying with freedom; the water was crystal clear. Betty had a great time picking shells along the beach with her parents; her father made a seashell necklace for Betty when they returned. It was beautiful, and Betty had worn the necklace to bed that night. She stared at the portrait, and her mother was a doctor. Betty could remember the day her mother left for Canada. Her parents got into a big fight; Betty's father didn't want her mother to leave. The government had already announced that the trilemma was coming, and nobody took them seriously until the visible signs started. Betty's mother was very devoted to her job.

"I've to go, Kelvin," Lily said as she packed her bags. "Then what happens to us" Kevin answered. "I'll be gone for just one day. I'll be back before you know it," Lily said as she opened the door. "Hey, honey. Momma will be back soon" Lily planted a soft kiss on Betty's forehead. That was the last time Betty saw her mother; she didn't come back the next day as she promised. Betty cried when the trilemma started, and her mother wasn't there to comfort her. Betty was so sad she crawled into bed, and she didn't speak for days; the trilemma was going to take everything; that's what the news says. Betty wished she could go to Canada and tell her mother how much she loved her. Betty watched the sky turn pitch black; it wasn't a surprise anymore. At first, Betty screamed whenever everywhere turned black until she got the hang of it. Everything had changed since the trilemma, Betty didn't have any friends anymore, and it wasn't easy to play with other kids because they were locked inside the comfort of their home. Betty sighed deeply; her only friend was Mrs. Brentwood. The older woman sat on the porch every evening, and she enjoyed reading stories to Betty.

The door opened, and Betty's father walked into the room. "Grab me a plate," Ethan said. Betty ran to the kitchen to get the plate. Betty returned quickly and watched her father pour out the mushrooms from his pockets. "Where did you find them?" Betty asked as she dug her teeth into the mushroom. "I had to walk deep into the woods to get this," Ethan replied. He poured the mushrooms into the plate. "Dad?" Betty wasn't sure of how her father would take it. "Yes, honey" Ethan was cleaning the mushroom. "Can we go see mum?" Betty asked. "I wish we could, honey. But we can't," Ethan answered. "Why?" Betty couldn't get under anything. "Come on, honey" Ethan patted the couch, and Betty ran to the seat next to him. "Di, you know why we are eating mushrooms?" Ethan asked the little girl. "Because we don't have food" Betty answered. "That's correct, but do you know why we don't have food?" Ethan asked. "Mrs. Brentwood said the plants are dying" Betty shrugged. "You're correct, good job Betty" Ethan smiled. "Something happened to everyone in the world, and it's our fault. Now the skies are no longer blue, the waters are no longer white, and guess what?" Ethan asked his daughter. "We don't have food, and we don't have any money," Ethan explained. "So we can't see Mom?" Betty asked sadly. "We don't have any money, honey. And if we are going to see Mom, we need money." Ethan explained.

"But I have money. Can we go see Mom with my own money?" Betty asked. "You have money?" Ethan stared at the girl in shock. "Yes, I have money" Betty ran to her room and returned to the living room with a familiar piggy bank. "I didn't break my piggy bank because we didn't have Christmas," Betty said to her father. "I can see that," Ethan answered. "Dad, can we break it together?" Betty asked with a smile. "Of course, honey. If that's what you want," Ethan answered. Betty dashed into the room and returned again with a hammer. "We are going to take all the money, and we are going to see Mom," Betty said happily as she gave the hammer to her father. "Are you sure about this, honey?" her father asked. "Yes!!" Betty smiled, she had saved up a lot of money, and they were finally going to see Mom.

Betty's father knocked the piggy bank with a hammer, coins and dollar notes spilled out from the broken pig. "Now we have money" Betty jumped around the room happily. "Let's count the money," Ethan replied. Betty sat on the rug "1,2,3,4,5,6,7,8...." Betty and her father counted the money. "Dad! We have a lot of money. We have 127!!" Betty screamed with excitement. Ethan had not seen Betty smile in a long time, so he enjoyed watching the girl. "We'll go see Mom tomorrow with this money" Betty wrapped the money in a clean napkin. "I'll keep this under my pillow, so the money doesn't go missing, and I hope the tooth fairy doesn't come for it," Betty said. "I think the tooth fairy doesn't come unless there is a tooth under your pillow," Betty's father answered. "But she takes my tooth from beneath my pillow. I don't want her to take my money. Dad, should we hide the money in the ground?" Betty looked outside the window. "Then someone who doesn't have any money would take our money," Betty's father answered. "That's true" Betty placed her hands under her chin. "So, what do we do?" Ethan asked. "We would keep it under the flower pot in my room. That way, the tooth fairy wouldn't get it, and then nobody will know it's there" Betty loved the idea. "I like that idea," Ethan clapped with excitement. Betty poured out the sand from the flower pot into a plate and put the napkin into the flower pot. When the napkin was safely in the pit, Betty poured the sand back into the pot. No one would know the money was in the pot. "I'm going to pack my bags," Betty said after they stashed the money. "Okay," Ethan smiled.

The following morning, Betty rushed to her father's room "Dad, wake up" Betty was wearing her favorite dress. Mrs. Brentwood fixed the dress with a needle and thread, and it looked brand new. "We are going to be late," Betty cried. "Good morning, Betty" Ethan smiled. "Good morning, Dad" Betty returned the smile. "Dad, hurry, we are going to be late," Betty said. "Okay, I'm going get ready," Ethan answered. Betty and her father had to walk to the train station; Betty saw a small girl who looked like her age sitting at the train station in dirty clothes. "Dad, is she okay?" Betty tugged at her father's sleeves. "I don't know. Maybe we should ask her," Ethan answered. Betty walked to the girl at the train station. "Are you okay?" Betty sat next to her on the floor. "I can't find my Mom," the little girl cried. "Where did she go?" Betty asked the girl. "When I woke up, she was gone," the girl answered. "I'm sure she will come back. I'm going to find my mom too," Betty answered. "Are you sure?" the girl wiped her tears. "My mom will be back soon. So, your mom will be back soon" Betty smiled. "Thank you" the girl gave Betty a tight hug before running away. "Good job, Betty" Ethan smiled and gave his daughter a pat on the back. "Come, honey, Let's ask the gentleman over there if he can get us a train to Canada," Ethan said. Betty rushed to where the man was sitting. "Good morning, sir. Can you sell me two tickets to Canada, please?" Betty asked. "Do you have any money?" the man asked. "I have money," Betty answered confidently. Betty laid her napkin on the table to show the man her money. "I'm so sorry, dear, but this won't take you to Canada," the man answered. "Why?" Betty asked, disappointed. "It is not Ethereum," the man answered. "Ethereum?" Betty and Ethan chorused. "Yes, the only money that can take you Canada is Eth," the man answered. "Can I buy ETH with my money?" Betty looked down at her money in the napkin. "The ETH is super expensive, and your money won't be enough to buy," the man answered. "I guess this is all a waste then" Betty was sad. "Come on, Betty, let's go home," her father said. Ethan and Betty tied the napkin. "Thank you, sir," Betty said to the man as they left the train station. "So we are not going to see Mom," Betty said as they left the train station. "When all this is over, Mom will be back home" Ethan tried to smile. "But this may never be over, and Mom may never come back," Betty cried. "Oh! Honey, don't cry"

Ethan gave his daughter a big hug. "Are we going to see Mom again?" Betty asked. "I'm sure mom will come back," Ethan assured his daughter. Betty and her father walked hand in hand back to the house. "Do you know what we are going to do?" Ethan asked on their way home. Betty shook her head and stared at her father. "We are going to write Mom a letter," Betty's father answered. "I don't know how to write one," Betty complained. "Well, Dad is going to help you, and we are going to make sure it gets to Mom," Ethan promised.

When Betty and her father arrived at the house, Mrs. Brentwood was sitting on her porch looking at the sky. "Good morning, Mrs. Brentwood" Betty ran up the porch steps to join Mrs. Brentwood on the steps. "Good morning, Betty. How was your night?" Mrs. Brentwood asked. "I wanted to go see my mum in Canada but the man at the train station said I couldn't use my money," Betty replied. "Oh! I'm so sorry, dear," Mrs. Brentwood said. "It's okay; Dad is going to help me write a letter so I can send it to Mom," Betty answered. "That's a very good option" Mrs. Brentwood was no longer looking at the sky. "I think so too. I'm going to tell Mom that there was no Christmas, and we didn't have a Christmas turkey for dinner. I will also tell you that you're my new friend, and the man at the train station didn't let me come to Canada because I didn't have ETH," Betty said in her rush. "You can also tell her that you go to the field to pick fresh flowers for me," Mrs. Brentwood added. "Yes, I can also tell her that I met a girl at the train station who was also looking for her mother. I told the girl that she was going to find her mother, and she stopped crying" Betty smiled. "I'm sure your mother would be so proud of you" Mrs. Brentwood smiled. "Thank you, Mrs. Brentwood. I will bring more flowers in the evening" Betty smiled as she walked down the steps. "Thank you, honey. You're such a sweet soul" Mrs. Brentwood smiled as she watched the girl run home.

Betty found a pencil in her drawer; she also tore a page out of her notebook. "Dad! Let's write the letter to Mom," Betty said as she sat next to her father. "Okay" Ethan laid the paper on the rug. "I want to tell Mom everything," Betty said with a smile. "Well, you might need another paper," Ethan answered. Betty ran to her room to fetch the notebook; she was going to tell Mom everything.

"Mrs. Brandon?" a young man walked into the hospital ward. "Yes" Lily could barely hear herself; she was exhausted. "You have a mail" the man handed her a white envelope. "A mail?" Lily checked the mailing address, and it was from her house in London. Lily's hands were shaking as she opened the envelope; it looked like a long letter from Betty. Surprisingly, Betty's handwriting was neat and clean.

Dear Mom,

Hi, Mom. I hope you are doing great? Is the sky in Canada also dark? I wanted to come to see you; there was no Christmas so that I couldn't spend any of my money. There was no Christmas tree, no Christmas cookies, and no Christmas turkey because the sky was black. Mrs. Brentwood doesn't have any flowers again because the sky is black. All her flowers died, now Mrs. Brentwood just has beautiful flower pots in front of her house. Mrs. Brentwood also loves sitting on her porch looking at the black sky, and I don't know why. Last night Dad and I made mushroom soup sometimes. I also went into the fields to fetch flowers for Mrs. Brentwood.

I wrapped my money in a clean napkin after I broke my piggy bank; Dad and I were coming to see you. But the nice man at the train station said I can only board the train if I have ETH. I told him I wanted to see you, but he said it was very expensive. I also met a girl at the train station who was looking for her mother, she was crying, but I told her she was going to find her mother. The girl stopped crying and gave me a big smile. Dad suggested we write this letter.

PS: Dad misses you, and I love you. Come home soon

A tear escaped Lily's eyes; she sniffled as she read her daughter's letter. Lily was so angry that she couldn't see her daughter. Maybe she should have stayed back in London. The hospital was becoming crowded, and there were no drugs to treat the patients. Lily sat with her letter and imagined how disappointed Betty must have felt when she couldn't come to Canada. Lily knew she had to find a way home, but she couldn't afford the ETH. Ashely said it was very expensive but could be purchased from individuals. Lily hadn't seen Ashely all morning, and she could only hope that the young nurse had not eloped with the rest of her money. Lily stashed the letter in her bag; she could hear noise coming from the ward, so she decided to check it out. All she could offer at that point were words of encouragement.

At the research center in Portland, Professor Nasir and his team were working tirelessly. "Sir, Can you come to have a look at this?" Leonard was staring at the computer screen. Professor Nasir walked to Leonard's screen. "What do we have here?" the man asked. "It seems like the UV rays are no longer dormant; they are attacking the human race," Leonard answered. "When you say 'attacking,' what are you implying?" Professor Nasir slipped his hands into his pocket. "I don't know, sir, but this doesn't look good. At this point, nobody would be able to go outside," Leonard answered. "I thought the BTC was safely installed in some part of the globe," Professor Nasir was pacing. "The BTC is very slow," Camille answered. "ETH?" Professor Nasir was trying to hide his anxiety. "Super expensive," Rob replied. "So, what are our options?" the Professor. "We have to find a solution unless, the UV rays will kill us," Leonard replied. "The human race cannot fight that battle," Rob said quietly. "Camille, how is Silvio?" Professor Nasir sat on a chair. "He's not finished," Camille answered. "How long do we have?" Professor Nasir was drumming his fingers on the table. "I don't know, but we really need a savior right now. This is going to be a fierce and gruesome battle" Rob stared at the computer. "Everyone listen, this is not a time to panic. As far as we are concerned, Silvio is the only thing that can work. We've been on this project for the past two years, and trust me; we can't give up now. It's going to be a long and bumpy ride, but we better get Silvio up and running before this war begins" Professor Nasir knew the team needed the motivation; if they were going to save the world from the impending danger.

"So, everybody, get back to work! Let's get this thing done and spend the remaining of our lives with family," Professor Nasir ordered. Everyone went back to work immediately. "Leonard, I want you to keep me updated on the activities of the UV rays. Let's hope we can build a resistance before they get too violent." Professor Nasir said. "Okay, sir," Leonard answered. "Camille, what's the problem with Silvio?"

Professor Nasir asked; Camille was one of the brilliant minds of the team, and she was also one of the best software engineers in the world. "I need to get the operating system up and running. Silvio is designed to generate solutions for himself with his artificial intelligence," Camille sipped from her cup of coffee. "If I hear you correctly. Silvio isn't the real thing, but he's the generating house?" professor Nasir stared at the screen blankly. "That's exactly what I'm saying; with his artificial intelligence, he would create a technology that is capable of fighting the destructive Intruders," Camille explained. "That's good. We needed Silvio up and running as soon as possible. If the violent UV rays break out, then it's going to be a disaster, and trust me, we don't want that," Professor Nasir inhaled deeply.

The Professor had been striving hard to find a solution with his team members since the day the team discovered that the ozone orb had disappeared. It was something that they didn't see coming, and it took the world by surprise. Professor Nasir leaned back in his chair and wondered how Silvio was going to become a reality. If he was being honest, he had his doubts. With the impending danger, there would not be enough time to run proper diagnostics on the program. They were flying blindly here, and the only thing they could do at that point was to trust their instincts. The UV rays could strike a person dead in an instant. The truth is that before the BTC was launched, Professor Nasir had a feeling it wasn't going to be successful. Creating an orb that would secure the entire universe could only last for a while, and if they were going to create something that would be stationery and regenerated, they had to produce a system that could recreate itself. That's was how the idea of Silvio was given life; Professor Nasir could only hope that the idea would fall through.

The ETH was created by the countries that were out of the woods; the ETH was an attempt to centralize the funds. Its main purpose was to eradicate the financial situation, but it could not achieve that purpose because it was too expensive, and the average man could not afford it. People were dying of hunger, and from the pollution, they couldn't get treatment; because producing drugs is hazardous to the already polluted environment. Nothing was working, and Professor Nasir could only hope that Silvio was going to be a success. Silvio is the only way out, and they had to make it work. "Rob, can you get me the BTC margin on the screen? We need to know the progressive development," Professor Nasir said. The image was projected on the big screen in the room. "It's wearing out," Camille said quietly. "It won't last for long. The orb is no longer advancing; if the fight begins, it's going to start from there" Leonard pointed to the screen. "None of this will happen if we get Silvio ready before then," Professor Nasir said. "Uh…. I don't think so. The UV rays have touched base somewhere in Asia, and it is recorded that over two scores are dead" Rob projected the image on the screen. The room grew silent as they stared at the screen. "Let's get something done before it gets to us," Professor Nasir said. "I'm stepping out for a while" the man walked out of the control center into the dark world. The world had grown so dark he didn't even know what the world with color looked like anymore. The problem was, Professor Nasir, didn't know if the world was ever going to be the same. It would take a miracle to restore the world back to its original form.

Betty was on the fields; she enjoyed picking wildflowers. Everyone thought they were gone, but Betty knew where to find them. One day, while she was walking Betty, found what looked like a cove on the field. It was an enclosed space, hidden from the harsh sunlight, and somehow the grass managed to remain green. It was Betty's favorite place; other children wouldn't come out to play because their parents didn't want them to get the soot in their nostrils and mouth. Betty had to leave home with a mask (that Mrs. Brentwood made for her). Betty was returning home with her basket of flowers when she saw lighting in the sky. It was so frightening; Betty ran home. When Betty opened the door of the house, a great thunder-struck and Betty dropped the basket in fright. "Dad!" Betty found her father in the kitchen. "Yes, honey" her father wrapped his hand around her. "Dad!! Something is happening," Betty said; there were tears in her eyes. Betty and her father walked to the living room and saw the lighting in the sky, the thunderstruck, and they saw a big tree trunk fall to the ground. "Dad!" Betty used her father as a shield. Ethan held the frightened little girl close "Come on, honey. I'm here with you" Ethan didn't know what to do. They stepped into the house, and Ethan drew the curtains close; they could hear the sound but couldn't see anything. "It's probably just for a few hours. We'll be fine," Ethan assured his daughter. "Are you sure?" Betty held onto her father's sleeves. "I hope so" since the trilemma hit the earth, Ethan wasn't sure of anything. "I have an idea. Let's play something on the guitar to take our mind off things" Ethan bought Betty a guitar when she was five. The father and daughter loved playing the guitar together. Ethan pulled out the guitar from their cases, "What song are we singing?" Ethan asked. "Let's sing our song" Betty smiled for the first time since she rushed into the house. "Let's sing our song then," Ethan agreed. The father and daughter played the guitar while singing their favorite song. The storm was raging outside, but Ethan was right; they didn't have time to think about it. When the raging stopped, everyone stepped out of their house to examine the damage done.

Ethan and her father walked out of the house; some of their neighbors were also outside. There were a lot of tree trunks on the floor, some person's houses were affected. The thunder destroyed a lot of things; Betty looked at Mrs. Brentwood's house. The flowerpots were broken, and her roof was no longer there. "Dad?" Betty tugged at her father's sleeve to gain his attention. "Yes, dear?" Ethan turned to his daughter. "Mrs. Brentwood," Betty pointed to the woman's building. "Stay here. I will go check on her" Ethan ran across the street. Ethan knocked on her door "Mrs. Brentwood!!" there was no response from inside. "Mrs. Brentwood, it's Ethan," he shouted. Ethan didn't get any response; he was beginning to get worried. He kicked the door open with his leg, and the door almost fell off the hinges. "Mrs. Brentwood!" Ethan started searching the house frantically, "Mrs. Brentwood!!!" Ethan saw something from the corner of his eye. The room door was slightly open; Ethan pushed the door open and saw the older woman sitting on a chair staring at the window. "Mrs. Brentwood?" Ethan moved closer and noticed that the woman's eyes were closed, and she didn't move. Ethan's heart stopped.

He stood in front of her and tried to feel her pulse. Mrs. Brentwood's hands were cold; Ethan held her wrist so he could feel her pulse; she had a faint pulse. Ethan scooped the woman out of the chair and carried her out of the house. "Betty, grab me warm towels," Ethan yelled as he carried the older woman across the street. Betty ran into the house, and shortly after, her father entered the house with Mrs. Brentwood in his arms. Betty grabbed many towels, and she almost tripped. There was a bucket of water by the bed;

Ethan soaked the towel into the bucket of water. Ethan was doing heart compressions with his hands; Betty was taught at school. She watched her father pump the woman's heart and listen for breathing. The routine continued until Mrs. Brentwood heaved a deep breath. Betty squeezed the water out of the towel and placed the wet towel on Mrs. Brentwood's forehead. The woman's eyes were still shut, but Betty could hear her breathing now, and that was a relief. After a few minutes, her eyes opened slowly. "Betty?" Mrs. Brentwood's voice was shaking. "Are you okay, ma'am?" Betty wiped the tears from her eyes. "What happened?" Mrs. Brentwood asked. "There was a bolt of lightning in the sky and loud sounds of thunder rumbling. And...." Betty was explaining when her father cut her off. "Shhh... let Mrs. Brentwood rest; you can tell her all about it when she wakes up" Ethan smiled. "Okay. Mrs. Brentwood, dad said you need to rest. I will tell you all about it when you wake up." Betty gave the older woman a big hug. "Let's leave her to rest" Ethan held Betty by the hand, and they left the room. Ethan could understand that his daughter was scared; the look on her face when he came out of the house with Mrs. Brentwood in his arm was something he wasn't going to forget in a worry. "Will she be okay?" Betty asked as they walked out of the room. "Mrs. Betty is a fighter; she is going to be fine" Ethan planted a kiss on Betty's forehead. "Okay," Betty sighed and looked out the window. She wondered if her mother was okay in Canada. Maybe the storm didn't get there; Betty wrapped her small hands around her father.

Professor Nasir had to call the Director and inform him that Silvio was ready. Professor Nasir noticed that the Director didn't sound as delighted as he expected, and he couldn't blame the man. Director Peter had been disappointed by several attempts to save the planet, none of it worked out. In the past three years, Nasir and his team have devoted their time and efforts to creating an AI that can solve this problem on its own. They had lost some of their team members during the project, and Nasir was going to make sure it worked. Silvio took their time, sweat, and blood. He was designed to be a highly functional digital entity that would be able to solve the world's problem. Professor Nasir stared at the screen, Silvio had to work, and there was going back this time. "Camille, are we ready?" Professor Nasir asked. "Silvio is up and running, and that's the only option we have left. So, I guess we are ready," Camille answered nervously. "It's okay, Camille. Everything is going to be okay" the rumbling thunder in the background planted disbelief in their hearts. "Let's get out of here. Our work here is done," Professor Nasir said as he cleared the desk. "Camille, can you do the honors of launching the program?" Professor Nasir asked. Camille inhaled deeply, and she launched the program, the team left the facility, but they could monitor all the activities of Silvio remotely.

CHAPTER THREE

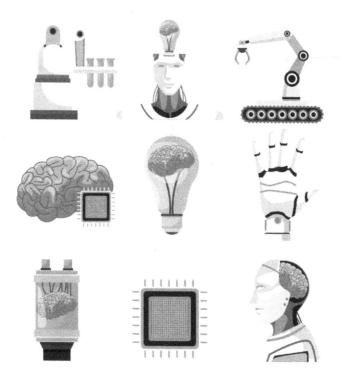

S ilvio saw the lightning in the sky and the thunder rumbling. Something inside of him told wanted to stop the thunder and the lightning. Silvio was in a dark room, and he didn't know how he got there. He sat in the dark for a few minutes, waiting for his eyes to adjust to the darkness. Silvio tried to turn on the switch, but he didn't get any light. Silvio groped in darkness until he found the door and walked out of the room. The air outside was chilly and was biting into his skin; everywhere was dark, but he managed to move into the city. The road was deserted, and many houses were without roofs; Silvio saw children sitting outside their houses crying. It was a disaster, and Silvio knew he had to do something. He walked farther into the city, the trees were dried up, and the lightning was scaring the children into hiding. Some parents were outside calling for their children. Silvio took a right turn and found a big field. Silvio looked at his meter. He was far away from home; he saw a little kid with a basket. Silvio scanned the image and realized that she was carrying a basket of wildflowers. The girl spotted him, and she started walking towards him. She was the first person that didn't have anxiety written on her face. "Are you lost?" the girl asked. Silvio stared at the girl blankly. "Are you scared?" the girl dropped her basket on the floor and stared at Silvio. "It's okay. I'm going to take you home," the girl spoke to Silvio quietly. "I'm Silvio," he answered. "Okay, Silvio. I'm Betty" the girl smiled. "Are you lost?" Betty asked again. Silvio was scanning her face; the girl was doing something with her face. The corners of her mouth were slightly raised, and Silvio tried to do it too. "You're smiling" Betty clapped with excitement. "That should be a good thing," Betty added. "I'm Silvio, and I'm going to save the world," Silvio replied. "Oh! I hope so. I want to save the world too," Betty sighed. "I'm going to save the world," Silvio said again. "Oh! No, Silvio. The storm is coming; we need to go somewhere safe. Let's go to my house." Betty picked up her basket and held Silvio's hands, and they started walking towards Betty's house.

"If you're lost, you can stay in my house for as long as you like," Betty said on their way home. "Mrs. Brentwood stays in our house because the storm destroyed her house. She almost died, but Dad ran into the house to save her. In the evening, we gather around to sing while Dad and I play the guitar" Betty talked to Silvio till they arrived at her house. Silvio was looking at the destroyed houses, the tree trunks on the road, and the environment was a complete mess. "Dad!!" Betty ran into the house with Silvio. "I'm here" Ethan was sitting in the living room. He noticed that the storm was coming, and he knew Betty would run home. Ethan and Betty had studied the activity of the storm, and the girl could read the disrupted weather perfectly. "Dad, this is my friend Silvio. I found him on the field; he was lost. The storm was coming, so I had to bring him home," Betty explained. "I'm Silvio, and I'm going save the world," Silvio said for the tenth time. "That's what he said when I found him" Betty laughed. "You're welcome, Silvio" Ethan smiled, his daughter had a sweetheart, and she really needed a friend. "I'll go check on Mrs. Brentwood" Ethan left the teenagers to play. "Chair" Silvio pointed to the chair by the fireplace. "Yes, good job. That's Mrs. Brentwood's favorite place," Betty answered. Silvio and Betty identified all the objects in the house before Ethan returned to the living room. "Betty, introduce your friend to Mrs. Brentwood while I prepare dinner," Ethan said as he walked into the kitchen. "Silvio, let's go say hi to Mrs. Brentwood" Betty picked up her basket of flowers. "Good evening, Mrs. Brentwood" Betty smiled. "Good evening, Betty. Your dad told me you have a new friend," Mrs. Brentwood said. "Yes, Silvio got lost on the field. The storm was coming, so I brought him home," Betty answered. "Now that's a good thing to do," Mrs. Brentwood smiled. "My name is Silvio, and I'm going to save the world," Silvio said. Mrs. Brentwood laughed. "Your friend is funny." "And smart too. Silvio can name all the objects in this room," Betty said proudly. "Now, that's very interesting" Mrs. Brentwood smiled. "I brought your flowers" Betty removed the wilted flowers from the vase beside the bed and replaced them with the new ones. "Thank you, Betty." Mrs. Brentwood smiled. Silvio scanned the woman on the bed; she was sick. "Are you sick?" Silvio asked quietly. "Yes, Silvio, but I will be back on my feet soon," Mrs. Brentwood answered. "Mrs. Brentwood is a strong woman" Betty smiled. "Thank you, Betty," Mrs. Brentwood smiled. "Let's leave her to rest. We can come back later" Betty and Silvio left the room.

Everyone had dinner when Betty's father was done cooking. It was a bland soup, but they had something to eat after Betty and Silvio cleared the table. Silvio had trouble cleaning the dishes, but Lily taught him, and he got the hang of it. Silvio was given a room in Betty's house, but before going to bed, everyone gathered in the living room and listened to Betty and Ethan play the guitar. It was a beautiful night; Silvio had to make it back to where he came from. He had enough time to think about what he was going to do to save the world. He had to save Mrs. Brentwood and give Betty good food and clothes to wear. When everyone was asleep, Silvio sneaked out of the house. There was no difference between day and night, and it looked the same. Silvio rerouted his GPS system to where he came from. He was going to find a way to save the world. Silvio walked back to the facility; it was the same way he left it. Silvio walked around the building and found a room with computers. Silvio couldn't sense anybody else in the building. He opened the room slowly, the light switch in this room worked, Silvio turned on the light. The room has the updated technology he needed to create the algo. Silvio sat in front of one of the computers and went to work. Silvio was fast and super easier; he was designed to have more reasoning abilities than humans. Silvio sat in front of the computer for hours, creating a program for the algo. It was the only solution to the trilemma, and the algo will be designed to solve decentralization, scalability, and security. The people were hungry and had no money because there was no decentralized system for their money. The algo was a revolutionary blockchain that was going to solve the trilemma. Betty walked to Silvio's room the following day, and he wasn't there. "Dad?" Betty ran to her father's room. "Yes, honey. What is it?" Ethan rose up from his bed. "Have you seen, Silvio?" Betty asked. "No, honey. He should be in his room," Ethan answered. "He is not there!" Betty's eyes were teary. "He may be outside" Ethan slipped into his slippers. Betty ran outside before her father finished the sentence. "Silvio! Silvio," Betty shouted, but she didn't get any response. A few minutes her father joined her in the search. They searched everywhere and couldn't find Silvio.

They returned to the house. Betty was sad. "Dad?" "Yes, dear," Ethan answered. "Do you think Silvio got lost again?" Betty asked. "I don't know," Ethan answered. "What if he gets hurt?" Betty asked. "Well, I hope he doesn't. Let's hope he will be back," Ethan replied. "I hope so too," Betty said sadly.

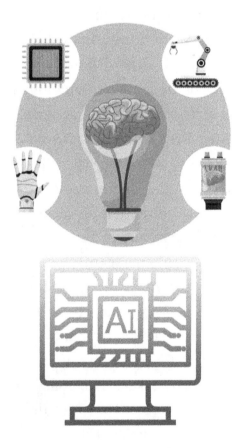

Silvio finished creating the algo at noon the next day. The algo was made of out carbon negative. Silvio had programmed wasn't the only thing that could help to save the world. Silvio needed someone to help with global warming. First, Silvio had to go back to Betty's house. She was his friend, and she may be able to help. Silvio left the facility and walked back to Betty's house, and he got to her house in the evening. Betty was sitting on the porch steps looking worried. When Silvio walked towards the house, Betty looked up suddenly and saw him. "Silvio!!!" Betty ran to meet him on the street. "Where did you go? I was so worried," Betty cried. "Did you get lost again?" Betty asked. "From now on, you'll stay beside me," Betty said as they walked towards the house. "Dad!!!! Silvio is back," Betty said with excitement. Ethan meets the two teenagers at the door. "Silvio, where have you been? You gave us a scare" Ethan was relieved that the boy was back. "I'm tired," Silvio said quietly. "Betty, let's Silvio rest. We can ask him all these questions later," Ethan said to his daughter. "Okay, dad" Betty wasn't excited, but she agreed. Silvio walked into his room to sleep; Betty went outside the house and sat on the porch. She had a lot of questions for Silvio, but she would have to wait for him to wake up.

Betty was reading a book to Mrs. Brentwood when Silvio woke up from his sleep. "Silvio," Betty waved at him. "Good evening, Mrs. Brentwood," Silvio said as he walked into the room. "Hey, Silvio. Everyone was worried; where did you go?" Mrs. Brentwood asked. "I went far away," Silvio answered. "Where?" Betty asked with curiosity. "It's very far," Silvio answered. "Why didn't you take me with you?" Betty asked. "It's too far," Silvio replied. "Okay, but next time when you're leaving, you tell someone," Mrs. Brentwood said quietly. Silvio responded with a nod. "I need to get some rest; you guys can leave now," Mrs. Brentwood smiled. Betty and Silvio left the room. "Did you find a way to save the world?" Betty whispered. "I think I've found a way, but I need help," Silvio answered. "I'll help you," Betty said eagerly. "Not that kind of help," Silvio replied. "But I still want to help," Betty insisted. "I can solve the poverty situation, but I need someone else to fight the global warming and pollution," Silvio explained. "When next you're going, I'm going with you," Betty replied. "I guess you can help with some other things," Silvio agreed. "But we'll have to tell Dad before we leave the house," Betty said to her friend, Silvio. "Okay," Silvio agreed. The two friends sat on the porch steps. "Do you think we'll have clear skies soon?" Betty asked. "We'll have clear skies soon, but we need someone to help us," Silvio answered. "I wish we could create somebody," Betty replied. "Create somebody?" Silvio looked at his friend. "Yes. I once made a robot for my science project. It was my creation," Betty answered. "That's right; we can create something to help just like I was created to save the world with my skills," Silvio replied. "Huh?" Betty was confused. "Thank you, Betty. You just gave me the best idea ever" Silvio tried to smile like Betty.

Silvio woke up the next morning with enthusiasm. Betty was also awake; the duo smiled as they met themselves in the hallway. "Dad! We are leaving," Betty said as they walked into the living room. "Be careful out there," Ethan replied. "Okay,"

Betty and Silvio chorused. "How far is the place?" Betty asked as they walked out of the house. "Very far," Silvio said. "I'll take my bike then," Betty wheeled her bike out of the garage. "Let's go" Betty smiled, she had no idea what plan Silvio had, but she was ready to help Silvio save the world. "Are you sure this is the place?" Betty asked when they arrived at the facility. "Yes. Come on, Betty; we don't have time" Silvio rushed into the building. Betty followed him carefully; the building looked spooky. Betty didn't touch the walls; she was afraid that something would jump out of them. Silvio stopped in front of a room then turned the doorknob; the room was filled with big computers, and Betty was dazed. "Wow!!! Is this real?" Betty asked. "Of course it is real" Silvio smiled; he was getting better at smiling. "Come, let me show you what I've been working on" Silvio projected the algo program on the big screen. "Wow!!!" Betty was amazed, but Silvio wasn't sure if it was the screen or the algo that made her eyes so huge. "This is algo, it's a revolutionary blockchain, but it's not finished. It still needs some NFTs," Silvio explained. "You're really going to save the world," Betty said in amazement. "But we have to fight global warming, and it's really important. If we can't fight global warming, then the algo would be a waste of time," Silvio explained. "So, what's the plan?" Betty asked. "We need a warrior that can fight global warming," Silvio answered. "Where are we going to find someone like that? Have you seen those lightning and thunders?" Betty couldn't believe her ears. "That's why we are going to need to create one as you did on the science project," Silvio answered. "Now, I like this; what do we do?" Betty rubbed her hands against each other. "After our discussion last night, I thought long and hard. We are going to create something like me, and he will be able to fight global warming," Silvio explained. "Something like you? What do you mean?" Betty stared at Silvio with confusion. "I'm an artificial intelligence," Silvio answered. "But you're just like me; how is that even possible?" Betty's head was spinning. "I don't know, but someone created me with human genetics" Silvio shrugged. Betty was in shock. "You're joking, right?" she couldn't believe her ears. "No. Why would I lie?" Silvio sat in front of one of the computers. "So, you're not a real person?" Betty screamed. "I can act like a real person, but technically I'm an AI," Silvio answered. "Do you have superpowers?" Betty thought she was dreaming. "I think I'm highly functional, and my performance is more than that of a real person" Silvio smiled. "I can't believe this" Betty leaned against a table. "Well, that's the truth. Can we get to work now?" Silvio asked. "Well, I need a minute to catch my breath," Betty inhaled deeply. "We just need to come up with something that can fight the pollution," Silvio said. "I know that! But I need a minute," Betty replied. A few minutes passed before Betty had her head back in the game. "Okay, I'm ready. What do you need me to do?" Betty exhaled loudly.

"I have a brilliant idea; we are going to create someone that will help us. I will start working on the programming; you can start working on the designs," Silvio said as he started typing some machine language into the computer. "Are you sure this is going to work?" Betty asked. "It's going to work, trust me" Silvio flashed Betty a reassuring smile. The duo worked tirelessly; Betty looked at the clock on the wall. "Oh! Silvio, we need to head back home now. If we don't, we will not make it home in time for dinner," Betty said as she packed their things. "But we are not done yet," Silvio replied. "We can't finish today. We'll continue tomorrow" Betty pulled Silvio out of the room. "Dad will be so angry, and Mrs. Brentwood would be worried," Betty said as she hopped on her bike. "But we are not finished," Silvio groaned. "Silvio, real humans, get worried when they can't find someone they love," Betty explained. "Oh! I see," Silvio replied. "I have a lot to teach you," Betty laughed. Thanks to Betty's bike, they got home before dinner. "We have you been all day. I was worried," Ethan said when he saw them. "Silvio and I lost track of time. Sorry, Dad," Betty apologized. "It's okay," Ethan replied. Everyone sat around the table for dinner; Mrs. Brentwood was strong enough to come out for dinner.

Betty and Silvio made a daily trip to the research center to complete their project. After a week of working tirelessly, Silvio and Betty completed the project. "What are we going to call him?" Silvio asked. Betty stared at the project for a long time "Kitsu," she said quietly. "Kitsu?" Silvio wasn't sure he heard her correctly. "Yes. Kitsu, it means smart fox," Betty replied. "Why Kitsu?" Silvio asked. "He looks like a fox, and you told me you would create something like yourself. You're smart, and the fox is smart," Betty explained. "I think I

CHAPTER THREE | 59

like it" Silvio smiled. "So when does Kitsu start working?" Betty asked. "As soon as you press that button," Silvio pointed to the button on the console. "I feel like something is missing, though," Betty said as she stared at Kitsu's frame. "What is that?" Silvio asked. "Kitsu is going to be a hero, right?" Betty paced the room. "Yes," Silvio answered. "He needs a cape, an arrow, sword, and accessories to fight global warming," Betty said with excitement. "Why would he need that? Kitsu has inherent powers," Silvio replied. "You don't understand, Silvio. Every superhero has one; Superman has a cape, Wonder woman has a shield, I think Thor has a hammer. The point is every superhero needs a weapon," Betty explained. "Well, what do we do? I can't make any of these things except you can make them" Silvio shrugged. "I know someone who can," Betty answered. "Who?" Silvio asked. "My dad. He's a good artist, and he can design the perfect accessories for Kitsu." Betty replied. "Okay. If you insist that Kitsu needs accessories, then we'll get him one," Silvio sighed. "If you want him to be considered a superhero, then he needs one," Betty squealed with joy.

"Dad?" Betty had been thinking of a way to tell her father about Kitsu. "Yes, dear" Ethan was cleaning the dishes in the sink. "Silvio and I want to take you somewhere tomorrow," Betty said, smiling. "Is it the same place you both have been sneaking to?" Ethan asked as he wiped the plates with a napkin. "Yes, Dad," Betty answered. "Okay," Ethan sighed. "Thank you, Dad, you won't regret this," Betty said smiling. "This better be good" Ethan loved watching his little girl smile. Betty was the only that gave him joy in the midst of the chaos. "Silvio, Kitsu, and I would save the world," Betty said with excitement. "Who is Kitsu?" Ethan asked. "You will find out soon" Betty ran to her room before Ethan could ask any more questions.

Ethan had no idea where the children were taking him, but they were both excited. "Dad, you'll need to ride your bike," Betty said as soon as they stepped out of the house. "How far is this place?" Ethan asked as he wheeled his bike from the garage. "I can't tell" Betty smiled. After a long ride, they stooped in front of an abandoned building. "Betty?" Ethan didn't like the look of the place. "Yes, Dad," Betty answered. "I don't think this is a good spot for kids to hang out," Ethan said as they walked into the building. "Relax, Dad. Silvio and I hang out here all the time," Betty replied. Silvio opened the door to one of the many rooms in the building, and what Ethan saw sent him reeling back. "What is this?" Ethan stared at the young teenagers in amazement. "How did you find this place?" Ethan asked. "Silvio was made here," Betty said as she walked towards her work desk. "What do you mean?" Ethan turned to the girl for more explanation. "I'm an AI with human genetics," Silvio answered. "Betty? What's he saying?" Ethan looked confused. "Silvio is not a real person, but he can act like a real person," Betty answered. "You've got to be kidding me" Ethan leaned against a table. "It's no joke, Dad. Silvio is super wise and can use his intellectual reasoning more than any real person," Betty explained. Ethan grabbed a chair to sit, he could feel the cold sweat breaking out from his forehead. "But that's not why we brought you here today, dad" Betty had a twinkle in her eyes, and Ethan knew there was more to come. He just didn't know if he was prepared for it. "Silvio and I have been working on a project that is going to save the whole world from the trilemma. We have created a savior for the entire human race" Betty was walking in front of her father. Betty's movement was making Ethan feel dizzy. "Stop pacing, Betty. Just get on with it" Ethan's sighed deeply. Silvio was standing beside an object covered with a plain white cloth. "Are you ready?" Betty clapped her hands, and Silvio took off the cloth. Ethan almost stopped breathing; he was staring at what looked like a fox. "Is that a fox?" Ethan was stunned. "No, Dad. This is Kitsu," Betty answered. "How is a fox going to save the world?" Ethan threw up his hands in the air. "Kitsu decided to fight the trilemma," Betty replied. "And you think this is going to work?" Ethan stared at Betty and Silvio in disbelief. "Silvio is working, so Kitsu is going to work," Betty said with conviction. "Okay" Ethan raised his hands in surrender. "We brought you here so you can make Kitsu look like a superhero," Betty explained. "I'm not sure I understand you" Ethan leaned back into the chair. "Kitsu needs a shield, a sword, and a cape," Betty answered. "Oh! I think I understand you now. You want me to design Kitsu accessories" Ethan stared at the realistic fox in the room. "You're sure this fox is going to save us from this chaos?" Ethan turned to Silvio. "I'm confident," Silvio answered. "Let's get work then," Ethan said as she rose up from the chair. "But I don't think

Kitsu will be able to use a shield," Ethan said. "Why not?" Betty sounded disappointed. "You have to consider his structure," Ethan answered. "How will he protect himself from the UV rays?" Betty asked. "We can design the cape to be a shield," Ethan suggested. "Dad, you're the best" Betty smiled. "I should have joined the team earlier" Ethan smiled; he was sketching Kitsu's inventory on one of the computers. "We wanted to make it a surprise," Betty answered. "You surprised me; that I can assure you" Ethan laughed.

"Silvio, are we ready?" Betty asked; she was anxious. "I think we are," Silvio answered. Ethan clipped the cape into its position. "Now, we are ready" Ethan admired his work; he made an orange cape with a gold accessory securing the cape. Kitsu looked like he was pulled out from a superhero movie and brought into reality. "Dad?" Betty was looking outside the window. "What is it, honey?" Ethan turned to look at his daughter. "I think a storm is coming" Betty was terrified. "Silvio, let's give Kitsu his first test run," Ethan said. "This is going to be Kitsu; the first battle" Silvio rubbed his hands against each other. Betty was holding her breath; she could hear the thunder rumbling outside. Ethan's palm was sweaty, Silvio pushed the red button, and the fox slowly came to life. He opened his eyes slowly; Betty noticed his eyes were blinking, and he looked around, familiarizing himself with the environment. "How is he going to know what to do?" Betty whispered. "You don't need to whisper, Betty. He has been programmed to identify a problem; the main purpose for his creation is the trilemma. He will do anything in his power to fight it," Silvio explained. Kitsu walked slowly towards Betty then stopped. "Betty," the fox said. "Oh!" Betty covered her mouth with her palms. "He knows my name?" Betty was in shock. "It's all programmed," Silvio smiled. "I hate to break this party, but is there a way we can get Kitsu to get out there. It's a tornado" Ethan was trying so hard to remain calm. "Tornado?" Betty ran to the window to confirm. "It's picking up," Betty said, and everyone rushed to the window.

Kitsu saw his friends rush to the window; he could see all that was happening from where he was standing. Something inside of Kitsu told him he had to stop it, Kitsu dug his feet to the ground, and he was in an elevated position. The whirring sound made everyone look in his direction; Kitsu shot out of the open window. The tornado was coming from the north, Kistu flew in that direction. The tornado was about to hit a house, and he could hear the kids in the house screaming and shouting. Kitsu landed in front of the house; he had just a few minutes to build up enough energy to stop the tornado. Kitsu braced himself for the hit, Kitsu put his hands forward. It looked like he was pushing down a big giant, Kitsu held his ground. The tornado could not go; further, Kistu held down the tornado till it fizzled out. The children in the house saw him hold down the tornado. "Momma, it's a fox," one of the children pointed at Kitsu. Before she could make it to the window, Kitsu was gone.

Betty was dazed when Kitsu flew back into the room, "What

just happened?" Betty's head was spinning. "I don't know, but I think we just found a solution," Ethan answered; he was surprised. The kids were correct; Kitsu was their only chance to save the world. "Kitsu, are you okay?" Silvio went close to the fox to assess him. "I think I'm okay," Kistu replied. "Do you know what this means?" Betty asked. "What do you have in mind?" Ethan knew his daughter was thinking about something. "If Kitsu can stop the tornado, that means he can stop the UV rays," Betty said with excitement. "That's true. But I don't think Kitsu is ready for that yet," Silvio answered. "What do you mean?" Betty asked. "He has to go into the space to fight the UV rays. We are not sure of Kitsu's performance on outer space," Silvio explained. "But that's the only way to fight global warming," Betty replied. "He can fight off the impending dangers for now till we come up with a solution," Silvio answered. "Let's all take a break" Ethan could sense the teenagers were stressed. "This is what we are going to do; Kitsu would fight the impending disaster for now while we work on some modifications," Ethan said. "That's a good idea" Betty clapped her hands. "I guess I have to get to work now," Silvio replied. "Is it possible to modify Kitsu's cape? If he's going to fight the UV rays, he going to need a shield from the harmful emissions" Ethan had a good feeling about this arrangement. "Well, I'm going to make his boots; he needs it. What do you guys think of the color black?" Betty smiled. "I like this, teamwork" Ethan raised his hands up.

"Kitsu is powered electrically, and with the electrical

neutrons flying around, I don't think that should be a problem," Silvio said as he wrote something down in his notepad. "The boots we designed are indestructible. They can go through fire, tornado, storm, water. They are high resistance" Betty was so excited. While there were talking, something hit the building. "What's that?" Betty could hear some rattling. "It feels like something is coming," Ethan answered. "What does that mean?" Betty was scared. "It is possible that the disappearance of the ozone layer has created a portal for other creatures from the transverse universe" Silvio was trying to put the piece together. "Silvio, you're not helping, and I don't understand a word," Betty cried. "You're saying the planet might have been invaded by aliens?" Ethan was trying to catch his breath. Betty heard a big bang, and she screamed. "Dad, this is not good," Betty cried. "I think we have to send Kitsu out there" Ethan rushed to push the button. There was a screeching noise in the hallway, and Betty was shaking with fear.

Kitsu leaned on his hind legs, and his eyes gleamed in the dark. "Wow! Betty, you've really outdone yourself. Diamond hands?" Ethan knew the girl was scared; he was only trying to cheer her up. "They shine in the dark" as the words left Betty's mouth, the power went out. "Oh! No. This is not a good sign, and I think I spoke too fast" Betty held on to her father. Silvio could see Kitsu moving towards the door from where he was hiding. There was a thermal camera in the room, something was hovering around the door, and Kitsu was moving closer to the door, growling. "Silvio, can you see anything?" Ethan's heart was racing. "Kitsu is close to the door; there is something out there," Silvio answered. "What is it?" Ethan asked. "I can't see it," Silvio responded. Betty was whimpering. There was a loud crashing sound followed by Betty's deafening shriek. Silvio could see what looked like a big dragon hovering around the room. "It looks like a dragon," Silvio said quietly. "I thought they were extinct," Ethan replied. There was a loud noise in the room. Silvio was glad he had a copy of the algo program on a flash drive that was in his pocket. Silvio heard somethings fall to the ground, Betty was whimpering in a corner. Ethan crawled to Silvio "What's going on there?" Ethan asked. "Have a look" Silvio gave Ethan the device. "Uh-oh, I don't know what this is, but he heading straight towards us. Duck!" Ethan yelled.

Kistu saw the creature walk into the room, one of the new modifications that Silvio added could make him blend into the environment unnoticed. The dragon like creature was heading straight his friends, Kitsu lunged at the dragon and struck the creature with his sword. There was a purple liquid oozing out of the creature's body and he fell to the ground with a thud. "You can come out" Kitsu cleared off the barricades. Betty was very reluctant, she wanted to hide behind the tables where no one could find her. "Come on, honey. It's over now," Ethan stretched out his hand to his daughter. "Dad, I'm scared" Betty cried. "I'm here with you, baby. You don't have anything to worry about" Ethan said reassuringly. Betty held her father's hand and he lifted her off the ground.

"If you're going to save the world with Silvio then you need to grow a tough skin" Ethan said, he gave Betty a gentle rub on her back.

"You guys need to see this" Silvio said quietly "What is it?" Ethan looked at the creature on the floor, it looked like a big dinosaur with wings. "What is this?" Betty screamed. "That's the same question I was going to ask" Ethan took a close look. "Why is purple, spurting out of his wound?" Betty was trying so hard not to hyperventilate, her breath was coming out in short gasps. Thankfully not all the computers were destroyed during the clash. Silvio rushed to one of the functioning computer after taking a picture of the creature to scan the image. "I was right" Silvio turned to look at the group. "Right about what?" Kitsu was lost. "There is a parallel universe and this thing you killed is from that universe" Silvio answered. "So you're saying more of this thing are coming?" Ethan pointed to the unidentifiable mammal laying on the ground. "I think some of them are here already" Betty said quietly. "Uh-oh. There is a truckload of them outside this building" Kitsu could see them rushing into the building. "Hide!!!" Kitsu shouted. Ethan grabbed Silvio and Betty by the arm and pulled them away. Silvio was able to grab the device on the table before they left the room.

CHAPTER FOUR

K itsu had to blend into the environment, it was the perfect disguise. But the dead mammal was in plain sight covered in it's purple blood. "Who did this?" one of them asked in a thundering voice. "They cannot be far away" another answered. Kitsu stepped out of his disguise before their search could begin. "Hey, guys. I don't think you're welcome here" Kitsu said calmly. "You killed our brother?" one of the mammal charged towards him, Kitsu hit his diamond hands against each other and the bolt of lightning hit the mammal. The intruder fell face down. "Whooo! I didn't know I could do that. Come on let's get this over with it" Kitsu jumped around the room with excitement. When the manuals saw another of their friend on the ground. They got furious, Silvio was worried that Kitsu would not be able to face the mammal all by himself. But Kitsu was having a swell time, he could feel the rush of energy in his blood as he struck every one of them down. Everything was happening so fast, Silvio couldn't get clear signal on the thermal device. The entire place was quiet all of sudden "Is he okay?" Betty asked. "I can't find him" Silvio answered. "What?" Betty was going to have a panic attack. "Okay, everyone grab some-thing and put it against the door" Ethan ordered. The trio tried to build a barricade "Are you sure this is okay?" Betty was skeptical. "We'll find a way out" Ethan had a problem believing his own words. "Where did he go?" Silvio couldn't find Kitsu anywhere.

"Is someone looking for me?" Kitsu was sitting on the window frame. "Kitsu!! I thought we lost you" Betty screamed. "I love these diamond hands. They rock" Kitsu showed off his diamond hands. "You gave us a scare out there, buddy" Ethan heaved a deep breath. "I'm fine. In fact I'm feeling fly" Kitsu smiled. "I can see that" Silvio replied. "We need to get Kitsu into space as soon as possible. We need to close the portal before we get more uninvited guests." Silvio said. "What are we going to do?" Betty asked. "We are getting Kistu into space. Open your ears, Betty" Ethan answered. "Are you ready, Kitsu?" Betty asked. "Whenever you're ready" Kitsu answered. "Okay, let's prepare to launch you into space" Silvio moved towards the door. "Uh, where are you going?" Kitsu asked. "To the control room" Silvio answered. "I wouldn't go there if I were you," Kitsu replied. "Is it that bad?" Ethan asked. "Bad will be an understatement. It's ugly," Kitsu answered. "I'll just wait out here for you guys" Betty looked scared. "We need some equipment in there" Silvio threw his hands in the air. "I will just clear the junk out, then you can go in" Kitsu disappeared. "Why does he do that?" Betty complained. "That's what Superheroes do. I guess," Ethan answered.

"The place is cleared. You can all go in now" Kitsu said. "Ahhh! Stop doing that it scares me" Betty cried. "I can help it. Tell Silvio, he made me like this" Kitsu smiled. "It was necessary" Silvio answered. "I would love to stay and chat but some creatures are creeping into our world through a portal" Ethan looked at the door. "We need to clear that out" Ethan was talking about the barricade. "I'll just take these out of the way" Kitsu ran to the door and cleared away the barricade in less than a minute. "Thank you, Kitsu" Ethan smiled. The group went into the control room, everything was back in place. "Kitsu, I really want to ask how you this, but I'm not going to ask" Betty said. "What's next?" Ethan asked. "Kitsu needs to know what he's dealing with" Silvio answered.

"This is the planet- Earth" Silvio pointed to the image on the screen. "But as you can see the planet is submerged by this darkness. Which as prevented the earth from having daylight, the darkness also transports UV rays directly to the earth because they are in close proximity with the earth. While you're working on closing the portal, we have figure out away to chase away the darkness" Silvio was snapping his fingers. "Can we locate the source of the darkness?" Ethan asked. "It doesn't have a source, a comet exploded and sent the earth into darkness" Silvio explained. "This is more complicated than I thought" Betty inhaled sharply. "There is only one thing I know that can fight darkness" Ethan said quietly. "Me?" Kitsu smiled. "Light" Ethan answered. "How do we make that work?" Silvio asked. "That's what we have to figure out" Ethan shrugged. "We can't risk sending Kitsu to the space twice. We have to solve the problem once and for all" Silvio replied. "Then we are going to need a very big light" Betty answered. "Big light? That could work" Silvio smiled. "Do you have a plan?" Ethan asked curiously. "If a blast created the darkness, a blast can create light. We just need to get earth out of the submerged darkness" Silvio answered. "What are you proposing?" Betty was confused. "A blast can push us out if this darkness into the light," Ethan and Silvio chorused. Kitsu clapped with enthusiasm "I love this plan already" he said. "Is it going to have any harmful effects? Betty asked. "We'll have to make sure it doesn't" Silvio answered.

"We have to apply enough force that shoot the globe out of the darkness" Silvio said to the group. "Kistu will strap the cannon to the earth before closing the portal" Silvio explained. "How will the cannon get to the space?" Betty asked. "We have to build it weightless so we can get it out there" Silvio answered. "How soon can we get him out there? We don't have much time," Ethan was hoping this plan would work. "I'm surprised another wave of mammal hasn't showed up" Betty's eyes were fixed on the door. "We have limited time. I suggest we get to work" Silvio said as she walked to the computer. "I just want it to be over" Betty groaned.

The group were able to complete the modifications, the designs and the production of all they were going to need. "Is that all?" Betty's heart was racing. "I think so" Silvio answered. "Kitsu are you okay?" Ethan asked. "Of course, I'm ready" Kitsu answered. "Okay, that's a good sign. We'll be monitoring your movement from here" Silvio plugged an earpiece. "Let's do this" Betty rubbed her palm against each other. Kitsu took a flight and the rest of the group watched him ascend into sky till they saw him no more. "Is he going to be okay?" Betty crossed her fingers. "Let's hope for the best" Ethan gave Betty a hug. "I've got visuals" Silvio was looking at the computer. Ethan and Betty turned to the screen "Is he there yet?" Betty asked. "It's a long travel, Betty. We have to be patient" Silvio answered. They watched the image on the screen. The GPS tracker was beeping "He's almost there" Silvio said quietly. Betty sat down on a chair, her legs were shaking. "Yes, he's in" Silvio said with triumph. "My heart almost stopped" Betty's heart was racing.

"Kitsu can you hear me?" Silvio spoke into the mic. "Yeah. I can hear you clearly," Kitsu answered. "How are you feeling out there?" Silvio asked. "A good experience but I think the darkness makes me uncomfortable" Kitsu answered. "You're a Superhero, you can handle it. Switch on your night vision" Silvio was pressing some buttons on the console. "Now, that's better" Kitsu could navigate through the darkness. "The minute you sense an incoming UV rays, initialize your shield system." Silvio said into the mic. "Okay, I got that," Kitsu answered. "I need you to fasten the cannon securely before you close the portal," Silvio instructed. "I'm on my way" Kitsu found his way around the dark and fastened the cannon to the globe. "That's done. Where am I headed?" Kitsu asked. "North, there is a lot of frequency coming from that direction" Silvio answered. "Copy that" Kitsu headed North and true to Silvio words he met the unimaginable. "Uh! Silvio, you didn't tell me this was a busy street" Kitsu could see the mammals in their large numbers trying to get into the planet. It was a whirlpool and they were jumping through. "It's a whirlpool Silvio. What do I do?" Kitsu watched from a distance. He knew his appearance was going to generate a lot of tension. "I don't know. You were the one who stopped the tornado, it looks like a whirlpool" Silvio answered. "I'm not sure they are the same thing but I'll do my best" Kitsu answered. "You better, because the whole world is dependent on you. You need to get back in safely before we shoot the cannon," Silvio knew this was a big task for Kitsu, but he was confident that the smart fox would pull through.

Betty was pacing the room, she was anxious. Betty wanted things to go smoothly, if things go well; Kitsu would save the universe and Betty would see her mother again. Betty didn't want to lose Kitsu too, she loved the smart fox. It only made sense, since she helped in bringing him into existence. Betty had given her all into designing Kitsu, and he was someone she was proud of; the fox was smart and hopefully the savior. She just wanted him to be okay.

Kitsu had to remain invisible to walk through the mammals,

it was important not to draw unnecessary attention to himself. If the mammals notice that he was there then it was going to chaos. Kitsu tried to blend in unnoticed. He had to make it through the whirlpool then shut the portal that was the only way out. Kitsu knew he had to deal with the mammals at the other side when he goes through the whirlpool but that won't be possible, if he couldn't make it. Something happened, there was a glitch in the disguise and a mammal spotted him. Kitsu was only a few feet away from whirlpool, "It's the smart fox" one of the mammals screamed. Kitsu knew is cover was blown when he heard the loud shout, some of the were gradually advancing towards him.

"Kitsu?" Silvio could hear the noise in the background. "Kitsu, are you there?" Silvio heard a screeching noise in his ears. "Is Kitsu okay?" Betty's heart was racing. "What's happening, Silvio,?" Ethan asked. "I think I lost him. I heard noises in the background before the com shut down" Silvio explained. "This is not good" Ethan said quietly. "Let's check the GPS," Ethan suggested. "He's off the radar" Silvio voice was almost like a whisper. "What does that mean?" Betty breath was coming out in short gasps. "I can't track him" Silvio answered. "I guess we'll have to shoot the cannon with Kitsu" Ethan said sadly. "Is there another way out?" Betty turned to Silvio for a response. She was hoping he had another option, but Silvio turned away without saying a word. Betty's heart broke when she realized that it was possible she would never see Kitsu again. Betty had grown to love the smart fox, he was like family now. Betty knows what's like to lose family and she wasn't happy about losing Kitsu.

As the mammals charged towards him, Kitsu instinctively hit his diamond hands against each other to protect himself. There was a big blast, as the bolt of lightning jumped from Kitsu's hands. He was sent spiraling into the whirlpool and the portal shut the minute he fell through it. Kitsu was faced down on the ground for a minute before rising to his feet. He had lost all his connections with Silvio during the blast. But Kitsu wasn't going to let that stop him, the mammal that went through the whirlpool had formed a circle around him. "Come on, guys! I've had enough with you people," Kitsu saw the first mammal charge towards him. Kitsu hit him with diamond hands and the mammal fell face flat on the ground. "Anyone else?" Kitsu raised his hands in challenging. He could tell the manuals were furious, but now wasn't the time to back down. Kitsu stomped the ground with his boots and the ground began to quake. The mammals could the feel the grounding opening up, Kitsu smiled as he slayed one of the mammals with his sword. "I would love to stay and chat but I've got a lot of work to do" Kitsu ascended up in the sky as the ground opened and swallowed the rest of the mammals. "Now, that is what I call a grand entrance" Kitsu smiled at his success. He knew he had to make it back to the research center.

"Is the algo ready?" Ethan asked. "Yes the NTFs are available on the algo" Silvio answered. "What is NFT?" Betty asked.

"Well it's called the non fungible tokens" Silvio answered. "It's cheaper and super effective" Ethan added. "What do you mean?" Betty asked. "You remember how we tried to buy ETH at the train station?" Ethan asked. "The ETH were expensive so we couldn't go" Betty answered. "Well, so the kitsune inu wouldn't be expensive; we are creating the NFTS so that everyone can afford it" Silvio explained. "So, you're saying, if we shoot this cannon ball, everything will be back to normal?" Betty had learned to live in the hard times, the thought everything being restored was like a dream. "Well, we'll have to plant the trees but ourselves" Silvio shrugged. "As long as we have a fertile soil that wouldn't be a problem" Ethan replied. "It's a pity Kitsu isn't here. He saved all of us" Betty had tears in her eyes. "Betty, things don't always go as planned. Sometimes there is a hitch in our plans but we just have to go on" Ethan was trying to console his daughter. "I just wish he was here with us" Betty sniffled.

"And where else would I be?" Kitsu sat on the window frame. "Kitsu!!!" Betty jumped with excitement. "We thought, we lost you" Betty cried. "I'll have you know that you guys can't get rid of me so easily" Kitsu replied. "I'm glad you're back" Silvio smiled. "I told you I loved these diamond hands. They always come in handy" Kitsu answered. Everyone in the room laughed. "It's so good to have you back" Ethan gave Kitsu a gentle rub. "Let's get rid of this misery since we are all here" Ethan said to the group. Betty held on to her father's sleeves as Silvio pushed the button. They could feel the movement, it felt like someone lunged the earth forward and it hit the light. Betty's eyes were closed "Come on honey, open your eyes" Ethan said quietly to his daughter. Betty wanted to remember every minute of it, she opened her eyes slowly and saw the clear skies. The world had been dark for so long, Betty didn't know what the skies looked like anymore. As she saw the blue clouds for the first time after the trilemma, a tear escaped from her eyes. Betty ran to Kitsu and gave him a tight hug "Thank you, Kitsu. You saved us" Betty cried.

CHAPTER FIVE

The clouds were high in the sky, there gust of the wind and fresh air filled the atmosphere. If someone paid close attention, the person may hear the birds chirping. The stench in the air was gone and was replaced with the smell of pines. Betty set a foot outside the research center and she screamed with joy. It was unbelievable, it was like their dreams became a reality, Ethan felt nostalgic, the thought of going out in the dark on the hunt for food came to mind. It was like someone switched on a bright light and the darkness faded away. "Is this real? This is not a dream, right?" Betty asked. "I don't think I would have gone through some much trouble for a dream" Kitsu laughed. "This is real, honey" Ethan answered. "I can't believe it, Dad" Betty replied. "I know, honey. It feels unreal" Ethan replied.

Living in the dark for the past three years, has left the world void, empty and without form. The world have been deserted by joy, happiness and love. The light had restored; hope, joy and happiness. All of the things that the darkness had stolen came rushing back. Everyone could feel it in the air, it was undeniable and obvious.

People rushed out of their houses, some were on the streets crying. Betty walked out of the building with the group, the smiles on the people's faces was enough proof that Kitsu saved them. As they walked into the street, the young boy Kitsu saved during the tornado shouted "Mom, that's the fox that saved us," the boy ran to Kitsu. The people parted and gave Kitsu a deafening round of applause, Ethan started a chant "Kitsu! Kitsu!!" The people loved him they were roaring his name as he walked past them.

Lily was trying to administer first aid to a patient when the night suddenly turned to day. Everyone rushed outside to see the sun high up in the sky. Lily's couldn't move, her feet were weak to carry her weight. She had lost all hope and she never believed she would live to see a day like this. The children were on the road shouting with jubilation. It felt like a dream, the blue sky was a sign of hope to the hopeless. Lily could see the genuine smile on the people's faces. The mere thought of seeing her family again sent flood of tears running down her cheeks. It was the only thing she had wished for in all these years of darkness. Lily felt she would never have a chance to right her wrongs; the light was giving her another chance, and she didn't know if she deserved it. Lily fell to her knees sobbing.

Mrs. Brentwood was in the room, Ethan and Betty were not at home. The duo would always rush off in the morning and come back exhausted. She was could hear people shouting, when she looked up the sky was clear. It felt like a dream, Mrs. Brentwood thought she had crossed over to the land of the dead. Everything was brighter and clearer, it was like a dream come true. She didn't want to be a burden to Ethan and his daughter; they had done enough for her. Mrs. Brentwood could not have asked for a better gift, she had endured the darkness for too long. Mrs. Brentwood was ready to escape into the arms of death.

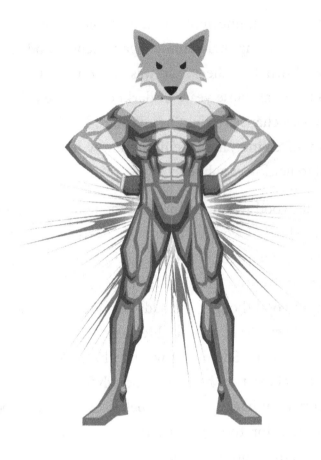

She heard running feet inside the house, the sound of those feet brought her back to reality, "Betty?" Mrs. Brentwood tried to stand up from her chair. "Mrs. Brentwood!!" Betty ran into the room with a bright smile like the clear skies. "What's all the noise about?" Mrs. Brentwood asked. "Kitsu saved us from the trilemma!!" Betty answered laughing. "Betty, I'm too old for your jokes" Mrs. Brentwood smiled. "I'm not joking, Mrs. Brentwood. Come see for yourself" Betty guided the older woman to the porch. "Oh! My goodness. I never thought I would see this day" tears were running down Mrs. Brentwood's face. "Don't cry. Things will get better now" Betty gave the woman a hug. "I can plant flowers now, and I don't have to go the field for wild flowers" Betty smiled. "You're such a darling" Mrs. Brentwood planted a kiss on Betty's forehead. Mrs. Brentwood mouthed the words 'Thank you' to Ethan who was standing a few feet away.

Peter could not believe his eyes, he stared at the clear sky without blinking. After several attempts to solve the trilemma, Peter thought it would never happen. He had given up on the possibility long ago. It was miracle, the trilemma had destroyed a lot of things but everyone was grateful for daylight and the fresh air. Peter inhaled deeply and exhaled.

Camille had to call Professor Nasir. He picked on the second ring "Professor Nasir, Silvio solved the trilemma" Camille said with excitement. "So, I heard" Professor Nasir answered. "Thank you for not giving up" Camille said with a low voice. "Silvio created a replica of himself. Only a brilliant mind can produce something or someone like that. Thank you for your hard work" Professor Nasir replied. Camille was lost for words after she ended the call. The trilemma was solved and that was all that mattered.

∾

The door bell rang and Betty rushed to answer the door. Ethan had organized a celebration dinner and everyone was invited. "Mom!!" Betty ran to the woman standing at the door and gave a tight hug. "I've missed you so much" Betty cried. "I've missed you too, honey" Lily was crying, she had not seen her child in three years. Lily had spent everyday of the last three years thinking about her family. Ethan rushed to door when he heard Betty scream. He stood rooted to the ground as he watched the two most important women in his life hugging. Ethan walked slowly towards them and gave the duo a hug. The last three years was tough on them as a family but thanks to Silvio and Kitsu there was a reunion.

Everyone was at the table when Lily walked into the house. "Mom! There are some persons I want you to meet" Betty pulled her mother to the dining area and introduced everyone. It was an evening full of joy and laughter. After dinner, Kitsu, Silvio, Ethan and Betty sat on the porch. "What's next?" Ethan asked. "I was waiting for that question" Silvio laughed. "We need more trees. The trilemma destroyed all the trees and we trees for oxygen" Betty answered. "We plant more trees then" Kitsu replied. "But I've never planted a tree before" Kitsu added. "I'll teach you" Betty replied. "Thank you, Betty. You're too kind" Kitsu smiled. "I have an idea. Since Kitsu is a Superhero, why don't we tell all of Kitsu's fans to plant a tree. That way we'll have more trees all over the world" Ethan suggested. "That's a great idea," everyone agreed. "I also have an idea" Lily joined them on the porch. "Mom?" Betty turned to her mother. "Yes, I want to be part of your group" Lily smiled. "You're welcome. But just so you know, we are going to be planting tree" Betty answered. "That's not a problem" Lily replied. "You said you have an idea. Let's hear it" Ethan said with a smile. "I know I'm new to the group. I think we should have Kitsu call all his Ambassador friends and tell them to join us in fighting pollution and poverty. I have friends in Canada" Lily answered. "I got a mail from America, France, Egypt and many other countries" Kitsu added. "I have pen pals from different countries too" Betty clapped her hands with excitement. "I think this is a very good idea" Silvio smiled.

"We'll be planting trees and fight against pollution and poverty at the same time. This is so cool!" Betty smiled. "Can we start tomorrow?" Betty asked "Of course" Kitsu answered. "That means I have a lot of letters to write. I 'll get started" Betty ran into the house. "We also have a lot of calls to make" Silvio rose to feet. "Let's get to work" Ethan added.

The team was able to call friends and families to join the fight against pollution and poverty. Kitsu and his friend were also able to start the plant a tree challenge; with over ten thousand trees planted in a single day. It was a successful event, everybody was careful with hazardous substance after the trilemma. They knew first-hand what negative impacts these hazardous substance can cause on the environment. Everyone was extra careful, the dark days were over and it was important to maintain the balance between night and day. Kitsu's job wasn't over, he had to fight against poverty and he also had to ensure that the people were keeping a clean and fresh environment. Kitsu continued to plant the trees with his team. The algo also encouraged the inhabitants of the earth to plant trees. The revolutionary blockchain was also interested in the safety of the environment.

Soon enough, there were green houses across the globe with people embracing and encouraging one another to keep the environment safe and habitable. Things were gradually returning to normal, only that this time it was better. Betty help Mrs. Brentwood revive her flower garden, it was very beautiful when they finished. Mrs. Brentwood sat on her porch every evening, enjoying the cool evening breeze. Betty still made a trip to the field sometimes to gather some wild flowers. Betty gave the flowers to some of her neighbors.

The team had meeting regularly, today was one of those days. Everyone was at the table except Betty. Silvio glanced at his wristwatch, the creaking sound of the door drew everyone's attention. "Betty you're late" everyone chorused. "I'm sorry. I had to water Mrs. Brentwood flowers" Betty answered as she slipped into her chair. "I want to thank everyone for actively participating in the fight against pollution and poverty" Kitsu appreciated the team. "We cannot stop now. But the current poverty situation have been brought to my notice" Kitsu added. "The wealth distribution isn't as projected; that is why we are going to distribute our special tokens to the entire glove population with the help of our friends" Kitsu announced. His statement was received with a deafening round of applause. "The special tokens will restore economic stability and regain happiness" Kitsu added.

Betty was excited, she loved contacting her pen pals to help with a challenge. Betty and the rest of the team made a list of the people they could help with the distribution. The team had grown considerably after the plant a tree challenge. The increase in number was a great improvement and the team could reach more people across the globe. They were going to make the world a better place with their concerted effort. The distribution started gradually and the people began to receive Kitsu's special tokens and soon enough the tokens were distributed all across the globe. Everyone had the special tokens, it was reminder of what the negligence of humanity cost them and it symbolizes hope to the less privileged. The whole world vowed to stay safe and protect the earth from all dangers and regain happiness.

BONUS CHAPTER

D ear Reader,

Thanks to this manuscript we truly hope you enjoyed and discovered in a soft and originally revisited manner how Algo was created and why it will truly change our future!

Did you know that no one in history ever solved the blockchain trilemma? Silvio did, but the real one!

Thanks to Algo now billion of people on the planet will

transact at low cost without polluting anymore our beloved planet! And it is happening right now while you read this!

Do not hesitate further, fasten your seat belt, and discover this amazing new blockchain that is revolutionizing the world! What else.... ah! did you enjoy Kitsu's adventures? then we kindly invite you to leave a spontaneous review!

Come to visit us at https://kitsuneinuasa.com/ and follow us on Social Networks to discover a whole new ecosystem!

www.ingramcontent.com/pod-product-compliance
Lightning Source LLC
Chambersburg PA
CBHW071301050326
40690CB00011B/2493